What Is This, If Not Survival?

By Ellie Sparks

QUILLKEEPERS PRESS

Book Cover Design by Quillkeepers Press

Edited by Stephanie Lamb

ISBN: 978-1-969601-10-1

Poems

Lunchbox Days	7
Blitzed and Blue	8
Teenage Tendencies	9
Proceed With Caution	11
Crestfallen Imperfection	12
Mum Says…	13
I Remind Her…	14
Raw and Reeling	15
Macabre Mutt	16
Still and Stale	17
Just A Regular Thursday	18
Mum Doesn't Get It	19
Bounties and Battleships	20
Ephialtes	22
Bug Bite Head	23
Manic Miscreant	24
Nefarious Nobility	25
Delving Into Diaphragmatic	26
Flatline	27
Mossy Caverns	28

Attempt #18 29
Thunderstruck 30
Begin Again? 32
Artful and Alive 33

It’s funny to watch yourself
tumble through the ether.
It’s also humorous
to try to predict your end.
But is this the way I should be
being?
Is this the way
my skull should bend?

I haven’t felt sentient
for a while now.
I’ve been suctioning existence
from Cabernet.
I know I should tease
my trying to carve this,
but dreamscapes dance
with doomsday.

I guess I’ll just
mull in this a while.
Embody a breed of stoicism.
Slumber until I’m an
edible carcass,

floundering into
self-deprecation.

I know you're trying, but
there's not much to say.
You see, I'm a gravestone.
I'm an obituary.
I'm just a being
birthed into   d e c a y.

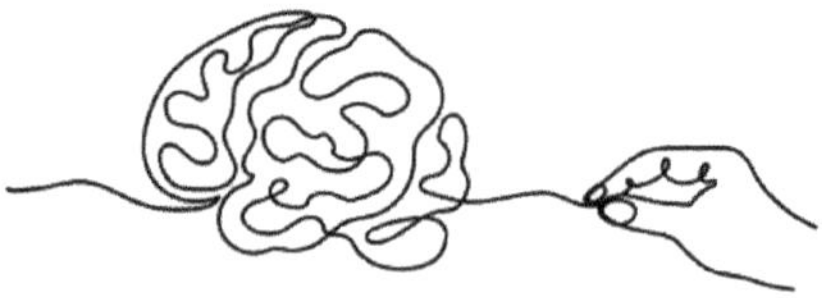

Lunchbox Days

I'm having a
quarter life crisis.
Don't blame my
hiatus.
I'm simply making
the best of this.
Sucking these
decrepit cysts.
Perfuming my laughter
lines in creviced bliss.
Since when did
lunchbox days
go amiss?
I'm cradling
the seared
abyss.

Blitzed and Blue

I remember

the first ounce of misery.

The initial

neurotransmissions.

The hovering warships.

Combat orbited around in

my bloodstream

until fibres blitzed in blues,

drenching my history

in hardship.

I spent the weekend

lazing in lifeboats

so languid,

whimpering in whittled

worship.

I remember preaching

to the skies

for some sapience

to leave me   less   famished.

Teenage Tendencies

I mourn everyone

I have ever cherished

and no *l e t t i n g g o*

can ever revive me.

I've been slumbering

in this

pit

for eons now,

churning up soot

from my

adolescent diary.

I've stepped upon

scales that have

c r u n c h e d

my cranium

down to my

spleen,

never to slurp these

haemorrhages

clean.

Those teenage tendencies

have never

absconded me,

just chart

idle isles in my dreams.

I wonder if I'll

always clamber

clumps of grime

in my bloodstream,

silence these

unholy screams.

I wonder if those I've

always yearned for

will ever

exonerate

me.

Proceed With Caution

Pick at me
with your fork,
but you'll just
scoff,
an inedible delicacy.
I'll get caught in your
windpipe,
and you'll have to
spew me
into sharp vapour,
like I'm a colossus
untamed.
I'm no celebratory
dinner.
In fact, I might just be
a chamber of
death.

Crestfallen Imperfection

I march to the melody
of my
own d e j e c t i o n ,
toss throwing stars
at the Mothership
of my own d e f l e c t i o n .
Have I ever
embodied more than
an obituary,
an epitaph,
a crestfallen
            i m p e r f e c t i o n ?
The medical panel
in my mind
reject my timely
r e s u r r e c t i o n ,
mutter concerns
about my
pallid c o m p l e x i o n ...

Mum Says…

Stop torching the wick
at both ends.
Your brain is already
a bonfire.
Do you want to melt
beneath perspiring skies?
Do you want to fade
into the dying

firmament?

I Remind Her...

I'm the heart of
identity —
eroded...
The collapse of —
colour...
Edited tragedy...
a temporary thrash.

Raw and Reeling

I ooze
bleeding sap
and pine needles.
Like the fir,
I am a staple of
solitude.
Like these spruces,
I taste raw in
midwinter's
gullet.

Macabre Mutt

It always feels like
the longest day
of the year,
the Black Dog
chewing
the crusted manacles
by my feet.
The funny thing is,
I just don't care.
My battleships are
bludgeoning to defeat.
I would tear my presence
apart,
if this could be made a
less
macabre
week.
My calendar is curling,
my respite is resting,
and for sanctity
does this
hushed
voice
bleat.

Still and Stale

Self-help videos
keep insisting I'll
meet the skyline,
but here I am,
lying on my back again
on a glacial Tuesday,
brain beaten as a board,
eyes vacant as a
midnight diner,
tears glassy as cloudbursts.
I can't bear to listen
to the compulsive lies.
They suggest I'm a
degenerate.
Don't they understand
that my
neurology bleeds thirst?
I can't just level up
and regenerate.

Just A Regular Thursday

These tragedies
croon songs of lament
and I blurt out
elegies of
excruciation.
Why does every
weekday
s l a y
me?

Mum Doesn't Get It

She says:
I've obtained some
meds for you.
Hopefully, honey,
they'll give you the
opportunity to b r e a t h e .

She utters my
cerebrum is noisy as
a grand prix.
Modern medicine
will be able to aid me.

I tell her I am a mariner
adorning a head-heavy anchor
on a deceased sea.
This betrayal is more
bludgeoning
than I can ever b e l i e v e .

Bounties and Battleships

I laze atop
my double duvet,
throat coarse from Mum's
taser-teasing treachery.
I want to hug hysteria,
letting this
bounty
bleed.
Why does she consider
that, for a single era,
I'll entertain elation
reclining before me?
She uttered it herself -
My cranium is a closed book,
so why will it ever
unlock?

It's a narrative swallowing
combustion, a vine-bound
folio adorned with a stopwatch.
Mum once said she didn't
want to make this
battleship
r
o
c
k.
Now I'm sputtering
salt water,
sullied
in shell-shock.

Ephialtes

I have died an
ordinary death and
here I lie
in the mausoleum.
Spectators crowd
around my crypt
like my epitaph
is scripture,
my corpse a
museum.
In a day or two,
they've lapsed, after
musing, *She's too*
young to be singing
an exit song.
I'm the only one
who knows I am
where I should have been
all along.

Bug Bite Head

They're like
conflated crystals -
the dissolving shards
of landfill
that droop from
my cranium.
One step towards
introversion
and I'll be cradling
mania.
Why do I always
shelve anvils
in this bug bite
head of mine?
Sometimes I feel
I'm just a revenant.
A sleepwalker.
A croaking
stain of time.

Manic Miscreant

I have more than
enough love.
That isn't *why*.
Mum keeps asking
me what I'm
'missing' and her
insinuation
makes me cry.
I'm not lacking in *affection*,
or craving *devotion,*
or seeking divine *assertion*,
or some brand of *diversion.*
Everything is as it
should be.
The problem here is *me*.

Nefarious Nobility

What a saintly
woman
this grief is.
What a tortured
princess.
She tries her
hardest to brutalise,
digging into the
catacombs of my
rest.
There's no
pretty peasantry.
She must be
the
best.
Her trilobite
treachery
is no practice
Test.

Delving Into Diaphragmatic

I read about
d e e p breathing
and tangle my time trying.
I recollect
dog-eared eyes
of Mum deflating.
Begrudging. *D y i n g* .
I challenge the
intrusive thoughts,
their density
temporarily frying.
I've never been one
to tinker with wiring.
I'm no damsel.
Just a girl, i d l i n g .
A kid, dreamscapes
d r y i n g ,
aiming to suppress her
constant crying.

Flatline

I buried a piece of
myself
under my pillow
last night, and the
bloodshed is still
gushing from the
soggy
duvet.
Why is it that
every time
I try to decapitate
a part of myself,
I end up
mentally
severed?
If only I could
adore the
crooked limbs
I adorn like
some sort of
celestial lover.
One of these days
my Mum might
find me flatlined
in a cul-de-sac,
torso-flailing,
moon dust
spurting
demise.

Mossy Caverns

I'm playing
hide and seek with the
mossy caverns
in my cerebrum,
trying to save myself
before depression
detonates me.
I just don't understand
how I can be so
sentient
one coronation,
then misplace the span-gold,
my tooth-marked throne,

my charred crown.
How is it that I pan out
this way
every nefarious night,
reversing on the freeway?
I guess I'll reside here until
he butchers my brain
and inevitably
hales
me
down.
I know far
too much
about myself
now.

Attempt #18

I press on with the
deep breathing, muse
that my spirit is defective.
Remarkably,
attempts are *selective*...

For the first time
in light-years,
my heartbeat hushes like
matter in a snow globe —
crumbs fallen to the bottom,
flakes dense and dissipated.
For the first instance
in breathlessness,
my limbs feel like they are
connected,
like my joints are no longer
frugally fated...
Sated...
Amputated.
I cry chariots.
Taste trophies.
Appeased. I've. Waited.

Thunderstruck

Have I washed away

the residue

of this rampant rut?

Perhaps I've just

stencilled luck.

I've plucked a

crocheted clover

as I've let calm erupt.

But, alas, Nazar strikes

once more.

I peel his waxy

retina off the

dissolving floor.

Gleam *thunderstruck*.

Have I evacuated

the invasion

of this oozing cut?

And even better…

Is my spirit

still

morbidly

stuck?

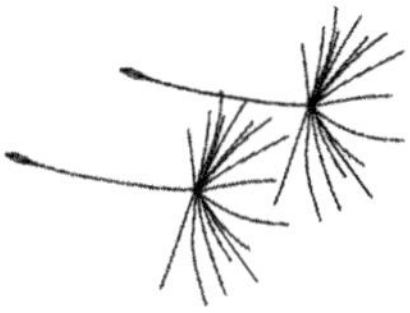

Begin Again?

I know it's no miracle, but
it feels like *something;*
like the icebergs in my
ironed out encephalon
are not currently clumping…

Now, what if
my nightmares start
dreaming; encasing themselves
in hot mercury, vengeance
fissuring? *Leaving…*

Distraction could even
ripple through my trembling
frame. Diversion glued shut,
ready for me to
begin again…

Artful and Alive

I bleed
confessional poetry
onto crusted pages
and the divulgence
issues my
drive.
I pen calligraphy,
purge my history,
list all the
reasons I might wish
to survive.
It's like a montage
of plush phrases,
these reminders
of the persistence
I demonstrate by
being alive.
I manifest more
ink blots,
considering all
the hope I
could
revive.

Mum asks me
how I'm doing
and I reply, *better.*
I'm no longer tightly tethered

to the shipwreck…
the tectonic plates
that elicit
torrential weather.

She smiles.
Knew they'd help,
the sooty capsules.
Those patient
testimonials
were exceptional.

I nod. *D e e p breathing*
has become
residual. I'm starting
to f e e l like an individual.
Perhaps her
proposal of
utilising this
timeless tactic
could embody a
righteous ritual.
Something
c o n t i n u a l .

I must admit,
though my curls
have sprouted tumbleweeds,
though my hours are
hexed by hostility,

though joggers still
adorn my legs,
hope has nibbled on my
cerebral empire,
has revived
my internal pyre.

This promise f e e l s
too g o o d to be true,
I whisper as I stare
up at the ether —
the tie-dye magnum opus,
ochre-split skyline
fissured
maroon.

I thank the grave
I will lie in
for it will one day
encase my cadaver.
But not for now —
this living could be luscious.
I'll taste the p e t r i c h o r
until it's over.
I've slow danced in
dense m e l a n c h o l y,
like all my mutuals.
Drained my dermis
of burst starlight.
But drama dims

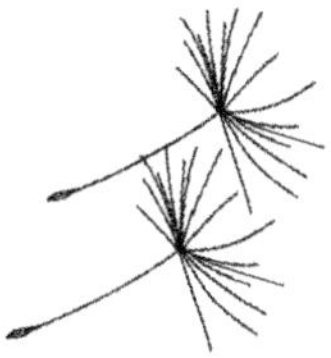

and the solstice
purges, and despite my
dysthymia, I'll try to
perceive existence
through my mother's
eyes.

Despite my parallel
perspective,

I'm h o p e f u l I'll

t r a v e r s e

a l i v e .

Ellie Sparks is a Creative Writing graduate who lives in the South of England. She started writing poetry to come to terms with her own mental health and has since turned her writing into a means to raise awareness about the complexity of mental health struggles and the importance of championing melancholy, even if it is just focusing on the little wins. She plans to keep writing about the subject of mental ill-health and wellness in order to help people feel less alone and more connected. She lives with her fiancé and two kittens, Shadow and Neo.

www.ingramcontent.com/pod-product-compliance
Lightning Source LLC
LaVergne TN
LVHW051923051126
851857LV00021B/2119
9781969601101